W9-CRC-859

HOW THE LEGISLATIVE BRANCH WORKS

by Christine Petersen

Content Consultant
Dr. Arnold Shober
Associate Professor of Government
Lawrence University

Core Library

An Imprint of Abdo Publishing
www.abdopublishing.com

www.abdopublishing.com

Published by Abdo Publishing, a division of ABDO, PO Box 398166,
Minneapolis, Minnesota 55439. Copyright © 2015 by Abdo Consulting
Group, Inc. International copyrights reserved in all countries. No part of
this book may be reproduced in any form without written permission from
the publisher. Core Library™ is a trademark and logo of Abdo Publishing.

Printed in the United States of America, North Mankato, Minnesota
092014
012015

THIS BOOK CONTAINS
RECYCLED MATERIALS

Cover Photo: iStockphoto/Thinkstock
Interior Photos: Library of Congress, 4, 7; Thinkstock, 9, 17, 28, 32, 38, 45;
Photos.com/Thinkstock, 12; Georgios Art/Thinkstock, 15, 36; Luis Alvarez/
AP Images, 20; J. Scott Applewhite/AP Images, 24; Purestock/Thinkstock,
30; Background Land/Shutterstock Images, 34

Editor: Heather C. Hudak
Series Designer: Becky Daum

Library of Congress Control Number: 2014944236

Cataloging-in-Publication Data
Petersen, Christine.
 How the legislative branch works / Christine Petersen.
   p. cm. -- (How the US government works)
 ISBN 978-1-62403-637-8 (lib. bdg.)
 Includes bibliographical references and index.
 1. United States. Congress--Juvenile literature. 2. United States--Politics
and government--Juvenile literature.   I. Title.
 328--dc23

                                                              2014944236

CONTENTS

CHAPTER ONE

Working for a Better United States

Have you ever wished you did not have to go to school? Maybe you find it hard to sit indoors on a beautiful day. Or you wake up tired and want to sleep in. Today every state requires children to be educated for at least ten years. But that has not always been the case. In 1900 about 2 million kids did not attend school.

Children worked long hours in a variety of jobs, including shucking oysters and tending babies.

Child Labor

Those children did not stay home and play. They were sent to work in factories, mines, and farms across the nation. Imagine if you spent each day of the school year crowded in a dark coal mine instead of going to class. Child workers in our nation's past began work at dawn and finished at dusk. Their work continued day after day. Young farm workers picked cotton or sorted seafood in the hot sun. In factories, children spent their entire days running huge machinery or bending over a tabletop sewing clothes. And child laborers were paid just a few cents per hour.

Poor families needed their children to work and make money to survive. Businesses could save money by paying children far less than they paid adults. And the United States had no laws preventing child labor. The results were terrible for everyone. Without an education, millions of working young people had little hope of getting good jobs as adults. Most would carry on the cycle of poverty.

At the Gorenflo Canning Company in Biloxi, Mississippi, child workers would arrive at the factory as early as 5 a.m.

Labor Laws

Some states had child labor laws as early as the 1840s. A law passed in Massachusetts in 1842 said children could not work for more than ten hours each day. But the country as a whole did not put child labor laws in place until the 1900s.

In 1907 the US Congress authorized the National Child Labor Committee to investigate the child labor issue. Photographer Lewis Hine began taking pictures of children at work. Hine had worked in a factory and understood the terrible conditions. His images stunned wealthy US citizens. Most people had no idea children were doing such difficult, dangerous work. Over the next 30 years, Congress tried to pass laws limiting child labor. They did research and talked to experts about how to protect worker rights. Members of Congress argued about the best way to address the issue. Eventually the Fair Labor Standards Act of 1938 was written. And Congress finally had enough votes to pass the law.

Today children in the United Stated are required to go to school. Laws limit work hours and define the kinds of jobs they can do until age 18.

So Many Rules!

We may not always like rules, but rules and laws are important in every community. They do not just tell us what to do and how to behave. Rules and laws keep us safe. They protect our belongings. They ensure everyone is treated fairly. Rules and laws allow groups of people to accomplish big goals that one person could not achieve alone. They are written down as a reminder for us to respect others and take care of our community.

Congress works in the Capitol Building in Washington, DC.

When children are old enough to get a job, they must be paid a minimum wage. These laws prevent businesses from treating children unfairly. They allow young people to earn money while finishing school.

Government Support

Concerned citizens helped shed light on the dangers of child labor. But they could not have changed the situation without support from the US Congress. Congress is one of three branches, or parts, of the United States federal government. There is also an

Splitting Power Three Ways

The US Constitution was written just after the American Revolution (1765–1783). The United States had been controlled by Great Britain. During the war, colonists fought to break free from rule of the British king and legislature. Writers of the US Constitution wanted to be sure no single person or group could ever take control of the US government. They divided the government into three branches. Each branch has unique responsibilities. And each has ways to limit the power of the other branches. For example, Congress must approve the people appointed to office by the president. The president may veto a law passed by Congress. And the Supreme Court can decide if a law is unconstitutional.

executive branch and a judicial branch.

The responsibilities of these three branches are defined in the US Constitution, which took effect in 1788. This important document is the highest law in the country. It explains how the government works and lists the basic rights all US citizens have. Senators and representatives in the legislative branch make the laws. The president leads the executive branch. The job of this branch is to carry out laws.

The Three Branches of Federal Government

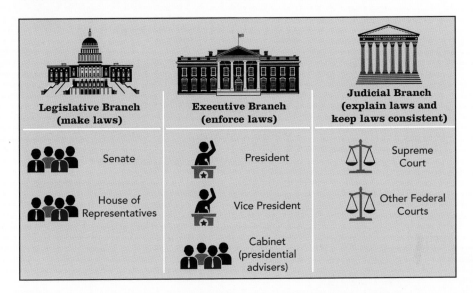

Legislative Branch (make laws)	Executive Branch (enforce laws)	Judicial Branch (explain laws and keep laws consistent)
Senate	President	Supreme Court
House of Representatives	Vice President	Other Federal Courts
	Cabinet (presidential advisers)	

This diagram shows the three branches of the federal government and the responsibilities of each. Does it match what you understand about them? How does the graphic help you better understand our federal government? What questions does it raise?

The judicial branch explains laws and makes sure they are used fairly.

The legislative branch is also known as Congress. The members of Congress have many jobs, but the most important is to pass laws that affect all US citizens.

CHAPTER TWO

The Houses of Congress

In 1787 a group of men gathered in Philadelphia, Pennsylvania. They had an important goal. They were going to write the US Constitution. The United States was still a very young nation. Just a few years earlier, it had fought a war to win its freedom from Great Britain. In the Constitution, the men wrote that no king or monarchy would rule the US people. Instead the United States would be a country in which

During the American Revolution, the United States fought for its freedom from British control.

citizens could elect their own leaders. If those leaders did a poor job, the people could vote them out in the next election. This form of government is called a republic. It was rare at the time.

Staying in Office

The president of the United States can only be elected to two terms of four years each. Congress does not have the same limits. If the majority of voters in a state believe a legislator is doing good work, that person may be reelected many times. Representative John Dingell of Michigan held office longer than any other US legislator. He retired in 2014 after serving 29 terms. That's 58 years! West Virginia chose Robert C. Byrd as senator in 1959. He remained in office for 51 years until his death in 2010.

Early Democracies

The United States was not the first nation to become a republic. Approximately 2,400 years ago, the ancient Greeks gave citizens voting rights. However, only adult male citizens could vote and participate in making laws. The Greeks called this type of government *demokratia*,

Pericles was an important leader during the ancient Greek democracy.

which means "people power." This is the origin of the word *democracy*.

By the 1600s, several Native American tribes living along the Atlantic coast agreed to become allies instead of enemies. This group of tribes became known as the Iroquois Confederacy. They wrote a Great Law of Peace. This document brought together warring tribes. It set up a form of government that allowed the tribes to live in peace. Each tribe sent

50 chiefs to join the Grand Council. Members of the council worked together, making decisions to help their people. Early US leaders studied ancient Greek democracy and the Iroquois Confederacy's Great Law when writing the US Constitution.

The Constitution and Congress

The Constitution set up our nation's new government. The US legislative system has two parts, the Senate and House of Representatives. This type of system is called bicameral, which comes from the Latin words for "two houses." The two houses of Congress work together to make laws. But they split up many other responsibilities of the legislative branch. This prevents either of the houses from becoming more powerful than the other. For example, the president selects new federal court judges. But the Senate decides whether or not to give a candidate the job. The House writes bills to explain how the US government will raise money in taxes. But the Senate must approve tax bills before they are signed into law. Congress's first

The US Constitution laid the framework for Congress.

law was passed in 1789. It allowed the government to set a 5 percent tax on goods imported into the United States from other nations. The tax money could be spent to run the government.

Congress Today

Voters in each of the 50 states elect people to represent them in Congress. The Constitution says each state will have two senators. These 100 men and women hold office for six years. Senators act for the whole state.

Each state also elects representatives in Congress. They speak for their home communities. The number of representatives for each state depends

The Great Compromise

In 1787 when leaders met in Philadelphia to write the Constitution, they also had to decide the structure of Congress. States with larger populations wanted more representatives in Congress. But states with fewer people worried they would not have an equal voice. The leaders found a compromise. They decided to elect two senators from each state, regardless of population. But larger states would have more representatives in the House. Each representative would serve a certain part of a state. In this arrangement, every US citizen is represented in the federal government by two senators and one representative.

on a state's population. California has more people than any other state, so it has the largest number of representatives at 53. Seven states have such small populations that they each elect one representative. The number of representatives from each state may shift over time as state populations grow or become smaller. But there must always be 435 representatives in total. Each representative is elected for a term of two years.

In 1988, the US Congress honored the Iroquois Confederacy for setting an example that helped shape the US Constitution. Congress wrote:

> *Now, therefore, be it Resolved by the House of Representatives (the Senate concurring), That—*
>
> *(1) the Congress, on the occasion of the two hundredth anniversary of the signing of the United States Constitution, acknowledges the contribution made by the Iroquois Confederacy and other Indian Nations to the formation and development of the United States;*
>
> *(2) the Congress also hereby reaffirms the constitutionally recognized government-to-government relationship with Indian tribes which has been the cornerstone of this Nation's official Indian policy . . .*
>
> Source: "H. Con. Res. 331." United States Senate. *United States Senate,* 1988. Web. Accessed July 19, 2014.

What's the Big Idea?

Take a close look at this quote. What is Congress's main point about the Iroquois Confederacy? Pick out two details used to make this point. What can you tell about the Iroquois Confederacy based on this quote?

CHAPTER THREE

How a Bill Becomes Law

How do laws come to be? Legislators spend time in their states. They listen to citizens' ideas and concerns. And they talk to one another about issues facing our nation. The president may suggest new bills, too.

US citizens can share their ideas with legislators by holding rallies or signing petitions.

The Capitol Building

Senators and representatives work in the US Capitol Building in Washington, DC. Construction on the Capitol Building began in 1793. It continued for almost 20 years. The building had a high dome at the center. It also had wings, or extensions, on either side—one for each house of Congress. In 1812 most of the building was destroyed in a fire set by British troops. The current Capitol building is much larger and even grander than the original. Visitors are welcome to tour the building and watch the House or Senate in session.

Starting the Process

It takes a lot of time, effort, and money to pass a bill into law. So legislators do not rush the process. They begin by sharing the idea with other lawmakers. If several representatives or senators agree an issue is important, they write a bill for it.

A bill is like the first draft of a law. Representatives give new bills to the Clerk of the House. The clerk keeps records of work done in the House of

Representatives. In the House, bills can be dropped into a box called the hopper. Senators stand up and announce new bills to each other.

The Name Game

Every bill gets a name. Bills from the House of Representatives start with the letters H.R. Senate bills start with the letter S. Numbers are added to the name to show the order in which the bills are introduced. For example, a 2010 bill involving health insurance began in the House. At that time, the bill was called H.R. 3590. Once it passed, the law became known as the Patient Protection and Affordable Care Act.

Committee Review

Once the new bill has been turned in, it is sent to a committee. Both the House and Senate have many committees. Each one focuses on a particular area of the law, such as education, employment, and the military. Most legislative work is done in committees.

The Senate Judiciary Committee meets to discuss issues such as the US immigration system.

Committee members discuss the issue. They do research to learn more about it. Committees also may invite experts to share their knowledge with them.

Not all bills make it through the committees. In some cases, bills may be tabled, or put aside. In other cases, committee members make some changes and report the bill. Reporting moves the bill forward for discussion and a vote in the House of Representatives or the Senate. A bill passes if more than half of the legislators in the house where it is being discussed vote in favor of it. But the bill has not yet become a law. Bills that begin in the House must go through this same process again in the Senate. Bills from the Senate are sent on to the House. Both houses must agree to any changes made to a bill.

Putting on the Brakes

In the Senate, each person has a chance to speak for or against a bill. Most comments are brief. Then the group takes a vote. Sometimes a senator may attempt to stop the vote by making a long speech. This act is called a filibuster. In a filibuster, the senator may speak for hours without a break. The filibuster ends if the senator stops speaking or sits down. Or the entire Senate may vote to stop the filibuster. If three-fifths of the senators agree, the filibustering senator must step down.

South Carolina's J. Strom Thurmond holds the record for the longest filibuster in US history. He spoke against the Civil Rights Act of 1957 for 24 hours and 18 minutes.

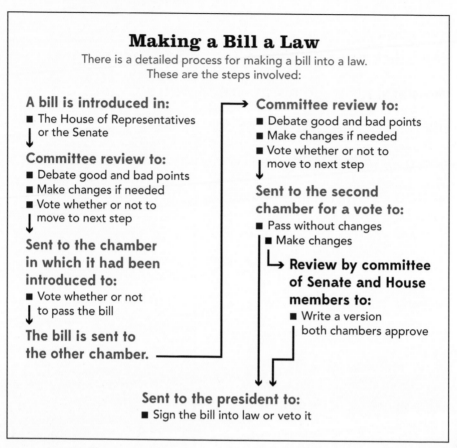

Making a Bill a Law

There is a detailed process for making a bill into a law.
These are the steps involved:

A bill is introduced in:
- The House of Representatives or the Senate

Committee review to:
- Debate good and bad points
- Make changes if needed
- Vote whether or not to move to next step

Sent to the chamber in which it had been introduced to:
- Vote whether or not to pass the bill

The bill is sent to the other chamber.

Committee review to:
- Debate good and bad points
- Make changes if needed
- Vote whether or not to move to next step

Sent to the second chamber for a vote to:
- Pass without changes
- Make changes

Review by committee of Senate and House members to:
- Write a version both chambers approve

Sent to the president to:
- Sign the bill into law or veto it

Making Laws

This diagram shows the steps for passing a bill into law. How does this information compare with what you have learned from the text? How are the steps similar to what you have learned? How are they different?

Becoming Law

Once a bill passes in Congress, it is sent to the president. The president can choose to sign the bill. Or the president can choose to veto the bill. Congress can block the president's veto if two-thirds of the legislators in each house vote to do so. Once the president signs a bill, it becomes federal law. The law must be followed by everyone in the United States.

FURTHER EVIDENCE

Chapter Three explains how a bill becomes law. What was one of the chapter's main points? What are some pieces of evidence in the chapter that support this main point? Check out the website at the link below. Does the information on this website support the main point in this chapter? Write a few sentences using new information from the website as evidence to support the main point in this chapter.

How Laws Are Made

www.mycorelibrary.com/legislative-branch

CHAPTER FOUR

Government Closer to Home

The US Congress passes laws affecting all people in the United States. But who is responsible for passing laws that affect only certain states? Each state has its own legislature. Like the US Congress, almost all state legislatures are bicameral. Each state, with the exception of Nebraska, has a Senate and a House of Representatives. A few states call the House by other names, such as

Nebraska is the only state that has a unicameral, or single house, legislature.

State taxes help fund services such as fire departments.

General Assembly or House of Delegates. The states'
Congresses try to resolve local issues that might not
be shared by other states.

Federal vs. State

In many ways, state and federal legislatures are similar.
Both make laws. State legislators also make choices
about how to raise and use tax money collected
from people in their state. This money allows the
government to provide services. Tax money is used to
provide education, roads and transportation systems,
health care programs, and much more.

Each state is broken into smaller districts based
on population. For example, Minnesota has 67

legislative districts. Voters elect one senator and two representatives to speak for their districts. Senators hold office for four years, and representatives have a two-year term. Other states have slightly different systems, but the goal is always the same. Lawmakers represent citizens in order to meet their needs.

Passing a State Bill

In the federal government, new bills and amendments move through one house of Congress at a time. Many states use the

Taking Initiative

In some states, people or groups can participate in making new laws. This process is called an initiative. The first step is to tell the state government about the initiative. The people who have the idea start by writing a summary of it. Then supporters speak to other citizens of the state about the initiative. They gather signatures, showing voters like the idea. The initiative may be sent to the legislature for a vote. Or it may be put on the election ballot. This gives voters the right to choose if a law should be made. Initiatives that get enough votes become law. They do not have to be put through the legislative process. The governor cannot veto an initiative once it has passed.

In Minnesota, a bill is sent to both houses at the same time.

same process. Other states use a different process. In some states, a bill is sent to both houses at once. It is read and discussed by committees. There are public hearings so citizens can share their thoughts, too. Changes are often made to the bill after these meetings. Then each house votes on the bill. If the bill passes in both houses, it is sent to the governor. If each house has a different version of the bill, typically both bills are sent to a committee. The committee is made up of members of both houses. They work together to reach an agreement. Then the bill is sent back to the House and the Senate to vote again. Once the bill passes, it is sent to the governor.

The governor can choose to veto or sign a bill into law. In most states, Congress can block the governor's veto if two-thirds of the legislators in each house vote to do so.

Governors have different veto powers than the president. The president can only veto whole bills. Some governors have nearly no veto power. Others can veto parts of bills, while some, such as Wisconsin's, can veto individual words.

EXPLORE ONLINE

The website below has even more information about state legislatures. As you know, every source is different. Reread Chapter Four of this book. What are the similarities between Chapter Four and the information you found on the website? Are there any differences? How do the two sources present information differently?

National Conference of State Legislatures
www.mycorelibrary.com/legislative-branch

CHAPTER FIVE

The Legislative System and You

O ver the past 200 years, US Congress has passed thousands of laws. Laws do not only tell people how to behave. They protect citizens' rights and provide services that make our lives better.

Most laws Congress passes are public laws. They affect all of society. The Magnuson-Stevens Act is an example of a public law. It is the main law governing US fisheries.

On June 8, 1789, James Madison proposed 39 changes to the US Constitution. All ten of the Bill of Rights were a part of his suggestions in some form.

A Changing Nation

The authors of the US Constitution tried to write laws that would be strong and useful for centuries to come. But the needs and concerns of the US people are not the same now as they were 200 years ago. That is why the Constitution is called a "living document." Like plants, animals, and other living things, the Constitution changes and grows over time. In this way, it continues to match our national values.

Any change or addition to the Constitution is called an amendment. Only 27 amendments have been passed in US history. The first ten amendments were made in 1791. Together these laws are known as the Bill of Rights. The Constitution describes how the US government works. The Bill of Rights has a different purpose. It states the most important rights and freedoms shared by all US citizens.

Seventeen other amendments to the Constitution have resolved issues early US leaders did not address, such as voting and civil rights issues. The original Constitution did not discuss the right to vote. For a long time, state laws governed the right

Electing African Americans

When the Fifteenth Amendment passed in 1870, Joseph Rainey of South Carolina was elected to the US House of Representatives. In Mississippi, voters chose Hiram Revels to serve in the Senate. These men became the first African Americans to serve in Congress. Mississippi and South Carolina were among the 11 Southern states that had lost the Civil War (1861–1865) just five years earlier. Their election of African-American legislators is an important reminder that change can happen quickly in government.

In 1971 the Twenty-Sixth Amendment set the voting age for all US citizens at 18 years old.

to vote. In many places, only white men could vote. Then in 1865, the Thirteenth Amendment banned slavery. African-American men obtained suffrage five years later under the Fifteenth Amendment. Women had to wait for the right to vote until the Nineteenth Amendment passed in 1920.

Congress's Other Jobs

It is easy to forget Congress has many important responsibilities aside from passing laws. Congress passed a law in 1789 to establish the national military. Although the president is Commander in Chief of those forces, the legislative branch funds the military. Only Congress has the power to declare war. Legislators manage the nation's trade with other countries. In their home states, legislators communicate with citizens and listen to their concerns about government.

Expanding the Nation

Congress has made it possible for the nation to grow. When the Constitution was written, the United States included only 13 states. All were on the continent's east coast. In the 1800s, legislators approved money to buy huge blocks of land from France and Spain. As a result, the nation now stretches from the Atlantic

A Bigger Nation

In 1803 President Thomas Jefferson made a deal with France. He wanted to buy a huge piece of French land called Louisiana. It stretched from Canada to the Gulf of Mexico and from the Mississippi River to the Rocky Mountains. Congress agreed to set aside $15 million for the purchase. President Jefferson also asked Congress to pay for a survey of the Louisiana Purchase. He sent 45 men up the Missouri River in 1804. They were led by Meriwether Lewis and William Clark. The team journeyed all the way to the Pacific Ocean.

to the Pacific. It even includes the distant states of Alaska and Hawaii.

Federal laws pay for highways and railroads. They ensure elderly citizens have the care they need. The government sets aside money for education. It creates laws to ensure our food is safe and to protect the environment. Congress also pays for scientific research to prevent or cure disease. Science funded by Congress builds new technologies and helps industries improve.

Some federal laws provide incentives for citizens to take action to benefit their own lives. For example, these laws may offer tax credits to people who own homes or go to college.

Every person plays an important part in government. You can participate by learning about issues that affect your community, state, and nation. You can write to lawmakers to share your ideas and concerns. And when you turn 18, you can register to vote.

In 1817 Representative John C. Calhoun asked the US Congress to provide money to build a system of roads and canals. He said:

> Let us, then, bind the republic together with a perfect system of roads and canals. Let us conquer space. It is thus the most distant parts of the republic will be brought within a few days' travel of the centre; it is thus that a citizen of the West will read the news of Boston still moist from the press. The mail and the press are the nerves of the body politic. By them, the slightest impression made on the most remote parts, is communicated to the whole system; and the more perfect the means of transportation, the more rapid and true the vibration. . . . Blessed with a form of government at once combining liberty and strength, we may reasonably raise our eyes to a most splendid future, if we only act in a manner worthy of our advantages.

> Source: John C. Calhoun. *The Works of John C. Calhoun, Vol. II* (R. K. Crallé, ed.). New York: D. Appleton and Company, 1854. Web. 26.

Back It Up

The author of this passage is using evidence to support a point. Write a paragraph describing the point the author is making. Then write down two or three pieces of evidence the author uses to make the point.

IMPORTANT DATES

400s BCE

Ancient Greece uses an early form of democracy.

1783

The United States wins the Revolutionary War against Great Britain.

1787

Early leaders write the US Constitution in Philadelphia, establishing the new nation's system of government.

1803

The US Congress funds the Louisiana Purchase.

1865

After the Civil War, the Thirteenth Amendment frees all slaves in the United States.

1870

Passage of the Fifteenth Amendment gives African-American men the right to vote.

1789

Congress passes its first law. It allows the government to set a 5 percent tax on goods imported to the United States.

1791

The states ratify the Bill of Rights.

1793

Construction begins on the first US Capitol Building.

1920

Women earn suffrage with the passage of the Nineteenth Amendment.

1938

Congress passes the Fair Labor Standards Act to stop child labor.

1971

The Twenty-Sixth Amendment sets the voting age at 18.

STOP AND THINK

Say What?

Studying how the legislative branch works can mean learning a lot of new vocabulary. Find five words in this book that you've never heard before. Use a dictionary to find out what they mean. Then write the meanings in your own words, and use each word in a new sentence.

Take a Stand

This book discusses elections and the terms people serve in state and federal legislatures. Do you believe there should be limits to how long senators and representatives can remain in office? Write a short essay explaining your opinion. Make sure to give reasons for your opinion and facts and details that support those reasons.

Why Do I Care?

The Constitution set up the US legislative branch more than 200 years ago. That doesn't mean it is unimportant to modern life. How does the legislative branch affect your life today? What might your life be like if Congress did not exist? Use your imagination!

You Are There

The authors of the Constitution wanted the US government to work well over many centuries. Imagine you could travel back in time to join them. You can give them a piece of advice about writing the Constitution. What is the most important idea you would make sure they include?

GLOSSARY

amendment
an addition or change to
a law

ballot
a system used to vote, usually
in secret

committee
a group that meets to discuss
and decide certain issues

compromise
to settle an argument by
giving each side some of
its demands

constitution
a set of laws by which a
nation or state is governed

democracy
a type of government in
which the people elect
their leaders

federal
having a unified
central government

initiative
a bill written by citizens
rather than lawmakers

legislator
a lawmaker in the Senate or
House of Representatives of
a federal or state government

republic
a nation in which the people
vote for their leaders

suffrage
the right to vote

table
to set aside

LEARN MORE

Books

Hamilton, John. *How a Bill Becomes a Law.*
Minneapolis, MN: ABDO Publishing, 2005.

Kennedy, Edward M. *My Senator and Me: A
Dog's-Eye View of Washington, DC.* New York:
Scholastic, 2006.

Websites

To learn more about How the US Government Works,
visit **booklinks.abdopublishing.com**. These links are
routinely monitored and updated to provide the most
current information available.

Visit **www.mycorelibrary.com** for free additional tools
for teachers and students.

INDEX

ABOUT THE AUTHOR

Before becoming a freelance writer, Christine Petersen worked as a bat biologist and a teacher. She has published more than 60 science, social studies, and health books for young people.